Be an ANIMAL DETECTIVE

Written by
Steve Parker

Illustrated by
David Anstey

B. Mitchell

A TEMPLAR BOOK

First published in Canada in 1989
by B. Mitchell

Devised and produced by Templar Publishing Ltd
107 High Street, Dorking, Surrey RH4 1QA

Editor Sue Seddon
House Editor Amanda Wood
Designer Peter Marriage

Color separations by Positive Colour Ltd, Maldon, Essex
Printed and bound by MacLehose & Partners Ltd, England

ISBN 0-88665-577-3

CONTENTS

Animal groups

Our world is teeming with animals. They live on the land, in lakes and rivers, on the seashore, in the deepest oceans, and high in the air. They are found in hot tropical forests and in icy-cold seas. Many are too small to be seen except with a microscope, like the tiny creatures floating in the plankton of the sea. A few are enormous, such as the whales that also inhabit the oceans. The main groups of animals are shown here. Each group contains many different kinds or species of animals. We still don't know exactly how many different species there are. New kinds are discovered regularly, in the ocean depths and in dense tropical forests. The world may contain more than 10

Birds. Birds are "warm-blooded," which means they use energy in food to keep their body temperature high, no matter what the temperature of the surroundings. Birds also have feathers and lay hard-shelled eggs.

Insects. An enormous group containing flies, fleas, bees, beetles, butterflies, grasshoppers and lice. A typical insect has a head, a middle part called the thorax, six legs (and perhaps two or four wings), and a rear part called an abdomen.

Worms. Earthworms are long and tube-like, with a body divided into many segments. Other types of worms, such as roundworms or nematodes, have no segments.

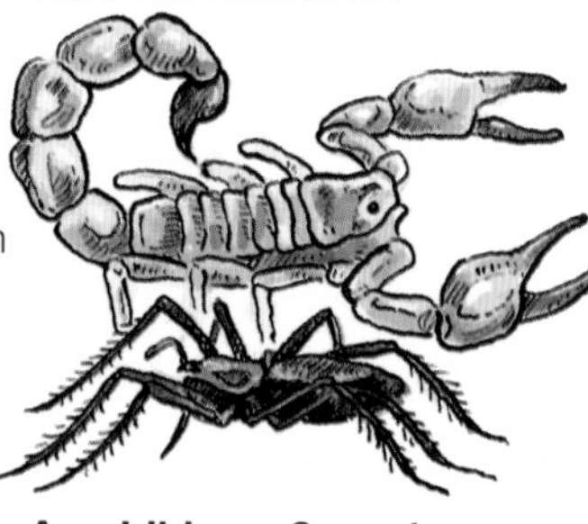

Spiders and scorpions. A spider has two parts, a head and an abdomen with eight legs. Scorpions are similar but slimmer, and have two crab-like pincers and a sting in their tail.

Reptiles. These animals lay eggs with hard shells and have a body covered with scales or bony plates. Lizards, snakes, turtles, tortoises, crocodiles and alligators are all reptiles.

Amphibians. Some frogs, toads, newts and salamanders live mostly on land. But all amphibians must lay their jelly-covered eggs in or near water, where they hatch into tadpoles. These breathe with gills at first, then with lungs as they grow to resemble their parents.

Fish. With their streamlined bodies, gills and fins, fish are one of the most easily recognized types of animals.

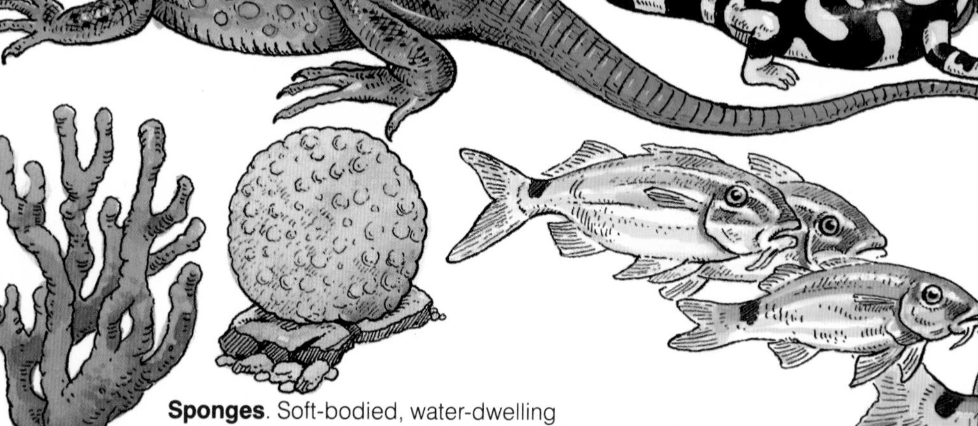

Sponges. Soft-bodied, water-dwelling creatures with no head or tail. They suck water in through holes and "eat" the tiny plants and animals floating in it.

million animal species. Most are insects: around one million insect species are known. There are more than 100,000 species of mollusks, about the same number of spiders and scorpions, about 50,000 worms, at least 30,000 different kinds of crustaceans, 20,000 fish species, 9,000 species of birds, and 4,000 mammal species!

Mammals. Like birds, mammals are "warm-blooded." Most have fur or hair, and they give birth to babies, rather than laying eggs. All mammal mothers feed their young on milk made in special glands, called mammary glands, on the chest (the word *mamma* means "breast").

Mollusks. Snails, slugs, oysters and octopuses are mollusks. Most have a shell, but no proper legs. Instead they have either a soft "foot" for crawling on, or tentacles like an octopus.

Crustaceans. Most crustaceans live in water or damp places. They have a shelled body and 10 legs. Crabs, shrimps, barnacles and woodlice are in this group.

Backbones

Animals that have a backbone are called vertebrates. Fish, amphibians, reptiles, birds and mammals are vertebrates. All other animals lack backbones and are called invertebrates.

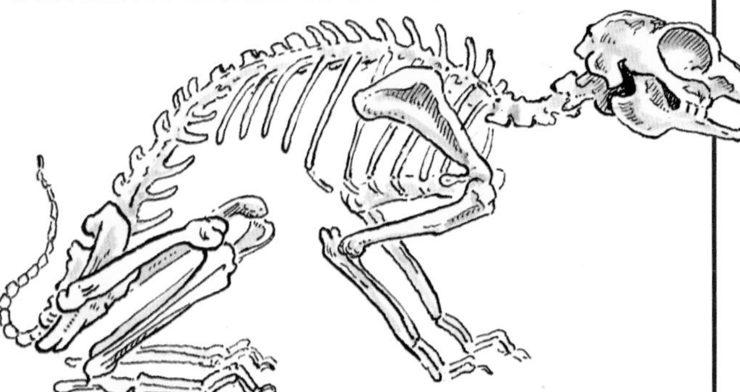

Warm or cold-blooded?

A warm-blooded animal uses energy from food to keep its body temperature warm, no matter what the temperature of its surroundings. Birds and mammals are warm-blooded. A cold-blooded animal cannot control its body temperature so well, and so it gets warmer or colder depending on its environment. Amphibians, fish and reptiles are cold-blooded.

Starfish and sea urchins. These sea-dwelling animals have a circular body plan based on the number five. A starfish has five arms. An urchin's five "arms" are folded over its head to make a ball shape.

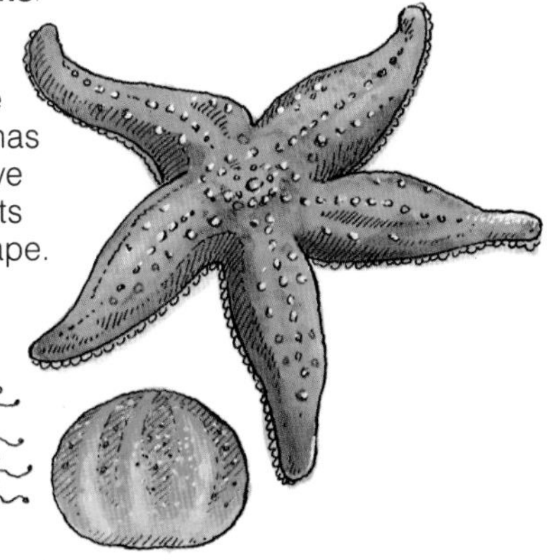

Jellyfish and sea anemones. Soft-bodied, water-dwelling creatures with dangling tentacles that catch and poison prey.

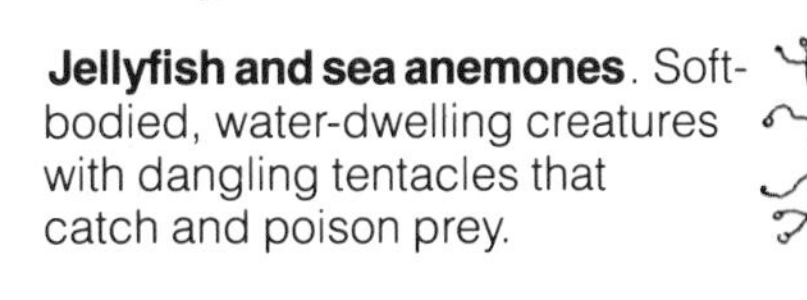

Eat, or be eaten!

*Animals eat an enormous variety of foods, from leaves, fruit and grass to bones, meat and eggs. But not every animal can eat every kind of food. Most animals are suited to certain foods only. They can be placed in one of three main groups, depending on what they eat. The groups are **herbivores**, which eat mainly plants; **carnivores**, which eat mainly other animals; and **omnivores**, which eat almost anything! The animal detective can study the clues given by an animal's body shape, limbs, claws and teeth, and work out to which group it belongs. Teeth are especially revealing, as you can read on page 10.*

PLANT-EATERS

Herbivores do not have to chase and catch their food. But they must be on the lookout for the animal-eaters. Plant-eaters such as deer, rabbits and mice tend to have good senses of eyesight, hearing and smell, to warn them of danger. Many, such as antelopes and kangaroos, have long legs for a fast escape. The plant eaters are the hunted of the animal world.

The springbuck. This southern African gazelle shows many characteristics of a plant eater. It can race away from a hunter at more than 37 miles per hour. In mid sprint it may suddenly leap 6½ feet straight up in the air, perhaps to confuse the pursuer. This sudden vertical leaping is called "pronking" or "stotting."

- Large ears pick up faint sounds
- Keen sense of smell to detect predators
- Large eyes on side of head allow all-round lookout
- Long, slender legs for fast running

ANIMAL-EATERS

Most carnivores are bigger and stronger than the creatures they feed on. They have sharp teeth and long claws which they use to catch, kill and cut up their prey. Some, like the tiger, stalk their victim with silent stealth. Others, such as wolves, track their prey until it is exhausted. The animal-eaters are the hunters of the animal world.

The barn owl. Owls are well equipped for swooping silently on mice, voles and other victims in the dead of night. Two forward-facing eyes give them binocular vision, allowing the owl to judge distance accurately as it swoops.

- Sharp beak to rip up prey
- Strong, sharp talons to grasp prey
- Large eyes to see in dim light
- Forward-facing eyes to judge distance accurately
- Soft-edged feathers for silent flight

ANYTHING-EATERS

Omnivores make a habit of eating almost anything, plant or animal, alive or dying or dead. Their body shape, teeth and claws are less specialized than the plant- or animal-eaters, and they survive mainly by being adaptable and eating whatever is available.

The badger. Badgers are strong, muscular animals. They can dig well with their large paws, and shuffle along at a surprisingly fast speed. They normally retreat to their burrow (called a "sett") when in danger, but will put up a fierce battle if attacked. They eat anything, from fruits and shoots to berries, insects, worms and birds' eggs.

- Long nose for detecting food and danger
- Small eyes give poor eyesight (smell is more important)
- Heavy claws dig both for food and to make tunnels

What do they eat?

Look carefully at these three animals. Can you work out the sorts of foods each animal eats? ***Is it a herbivore, a carnivore, or an omnivore?***

Spectacled bear. This heavily-built, muscular animal from South America has powerful yet blunt claws, small eyes, but a keen sense of smell.

Chevrotain. A dog-sized animal from South East Asia, the chevrotain has a sensitive snout, spindly legs, large eyes on the side of its head and large ears.

Genet. The African genet has forward-facing eyes, sharp teeth, and a lithe, athletic-looking body. Its sharp claws are kept withdrawn in their toe sheaths until needed.

ANSWERS

SPECTACLED BEAR
More like a badger than a dog or a deer, this bear is adaptable enough to eat almost anything it can find: fruits, roots, shoots, insects, and even small farm animals and deer. It is an omnivore.

CHEVROTAIN
The delicate chevrotain can hear and see well to detect danger. Its slim legs carry it quickly through the undergrowth of its rainforest home. It is a herbivore.

GENET
The genet is superbly equipped for hunting, with its sharp claws and teeth, and forward-facing eyes to judge the distance of its pounce. It is a carnivore.

Tooth clues

Animals must eat in order to stay alive. Teeth are for eating, and so they are tremendously important to their owner. They also tell the animal detective an enormous amount about the sorts of food an animal eats, and about its lifestyle. In addition, teeth are so hard that they do not rot away quickly when an animal dies. They may turn to stone, becoming fossils that last for millions of years. Much of our knowledge of dinosaurs and prehistoric humans comes from looking at fossils of their teeth.

MEAT TO EAT

Meat-eating carnivores must first catch and then eat their food. Animals such as the wildcat (above) and weasel have long, spear-like *canine* teeth, to hold onto struggling prey and tear its flesh. Large, back teeth have sharp ridges for cutting and chopping meat, gristle and bone.

- Long, sharp, canine teeth for grabbing and tearing
- Strong, ridged teeth for slicing and chopping

What, no teeth?

This animal is a puzzle. It has no teeth! It does have a long, sensitive nose, a long, sticky tongue, and huge front claws. ***What does it eat?*** *Perhaps it sniffs out very small food, picks it up with its tacky tongue and swallows it whole, without chewing. Maybe the claws are used to dig for food.*

THE FISH DISH

Fish are slippery and difficult to catch! Fish-eating carnivores, such as the shark (above) and the crocodile, usually have long rows of small, pointed teeth which help the animal to hold on to its shiny, squirming meal.

- Rows of sharp, peg-like teeth

GRAZING ON GRASS

Grasses and leaves are not rich in food value. Herbivores must eat lots of plant food, and chew it thoroughly, to obtain enough nourishment. Zebras (above) and buffaloes have small front teeth for "grass-cutting," and broad, flat back teeth for grinding their food.

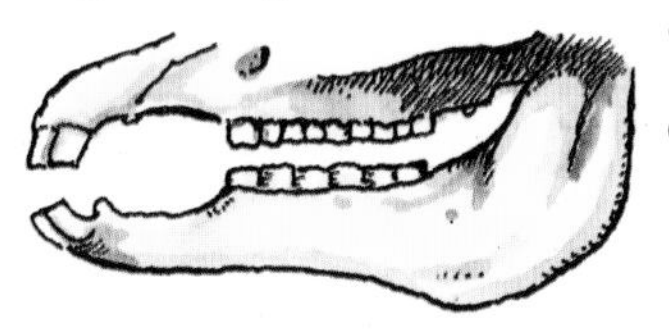

- Small teeth for cropping grass and leaves
- Large, flat teeth for chewing plant food

Dinner time

Here are three animals showing their teeth! And here are three meals that they might eat. ***Can you match each diner to its dinner?***

Look in the mirror

Give yourself a broad smile in the mirror. **Are your teeth specialized for a certain kind of food, like the animals shown here?** If not, what do you think this means?

ANSWERS

WHAT, NO TEETH?

The strange, toothless animal is an ant eater. It uses its claws to break open the nests of ants and termites. The ants stick to its tongue and are then swallowed whole.

DINNER TIME

Killer whale. This mammal (not a fish) has rows of small, sharp teeth, ideal for catching slippery customers such as fish – and squid!

Roe deer. Deer have small "grass-cutting" teeth at the front of the mouth, and large flat crushing teeth at the back, typical of a herbivore – and just right for eating juicy, young shoots!

Mongoose. The sharp *canine* teeth at the front, and the strong, ridges "slicers" at the back, point to a carnivore. Mongooses kill and eat snakes, but also catch and consume small animals, including mice and lizards.

LOOK IN THE MIRROR . . .

Human teeth are those of an omnivore.

Arms, legs and tails

For the animal detective, the shape of a creature's arms and legs give important clues about the way it lives. Long legs usually mean a fast runner (see page 8) while short, stumpy legs carry a heavy body. Arms and legs can also be specialized in other ways, as the creatures on this page show. After studying the clues, can you pair each of these three animals with a similar animal in the 'Match the animal' panel below?

KANGAROO

The kangaroo's legs are much longer and more muscular than its arms. People say that a kangaroo "hops," but it does not really "hop" like you, on one leg. It jumps with both legs together. A large kangaroo can bound along at 31 miles per hour and leap over fences 10 feet high.

SWIFT

A bird's "arms" are very special – they are wings, used for flying. The wing-flapping muscles, in the chest, are large and strong. Feathers make a light, broad surface to push against the air. The swift is well named, since it can fly at 93 miles per hour!

Match the animal

Look at these animals. Their legs, feet or arms are specialized for the way they live. Match each one to a similar animal on this page.

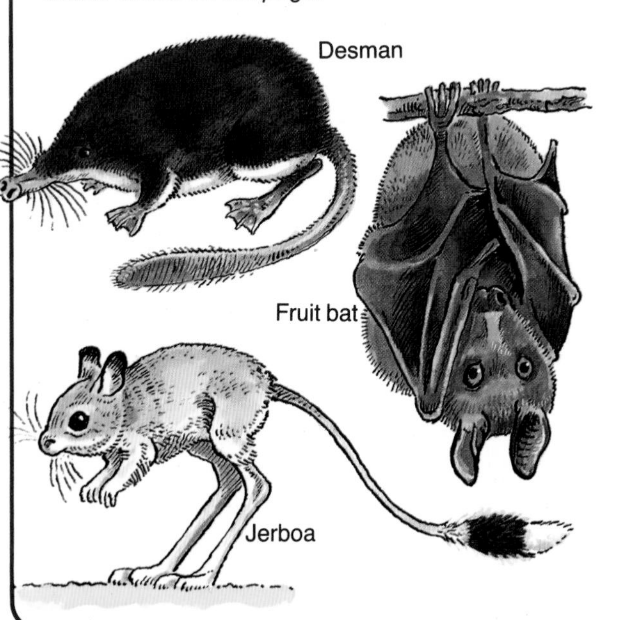

OTTER

The otter, an expert swimmer, has webbed paws with flaps of skin between the fingers and toes. This sort of design gives a large area to push against water. The otter also has waterproof fur and it can close its ears and nostrils under water.

Whose tail?

These three animals have become separated from their tails. Whose tail is which? Besides the size and color of the tail, look at what the animal is doing, and imagine how a tail could help it. Then trace each tail onto thick paper or thin card, color it and cut it out. ***Match the tails to the animals to see if you were right.***

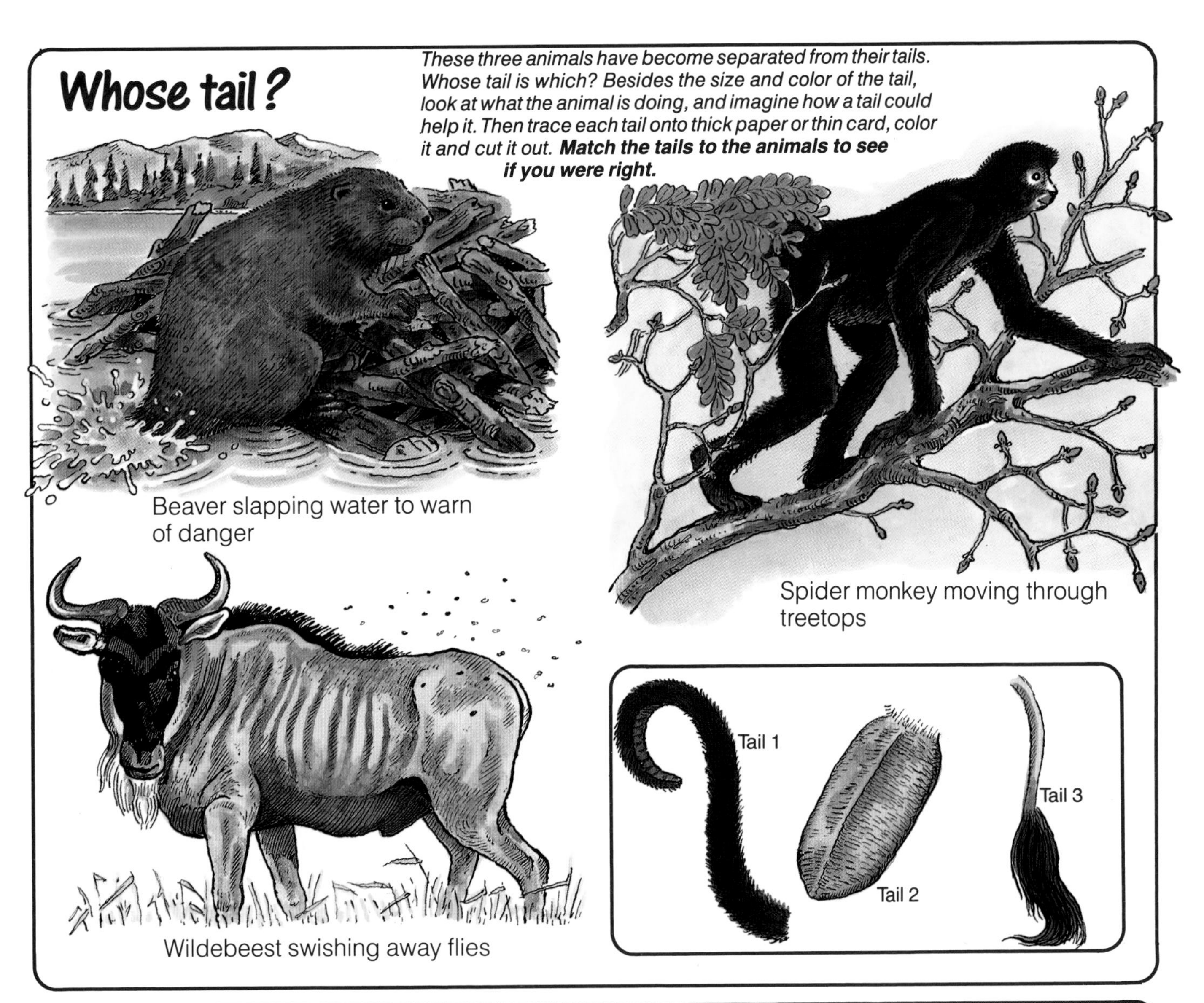

Beaver slapping water to warn of danger

Spider monkey moving through treetops

Wildebeest swishing away flies

ANSWERS

MATCH THE ANIMAL

The desert-dwelling jerboa moves in the same way as the kangaroo, by jumping on its powerful back legs. And, like the kangaroo, the jerboa uses its tail to lean on when standing still, and to keep its balance when leaping.

The desman has webbed feet like the otter, for fast swimming and diving in streams. It lives in water, eating small shrimps, water snails and water insects. It is a relative of the mole.

The fruit bat (also called a flying fox) has "arms" that are specialized as wings, like a bird. But a bat's wing is made of thin, leathery skin held out by the long, thin bones of its fingers.

WHOSE TAIL?

The **beaver's** tail is number 2. It is flat and scaly, and makes a loud "smack" when slapped onto the water's surface. This sound warns other family members of danger. The tail is also used for fast swimming and to steer under water.

The **spider monkey's** tail is number 1. It is *prehensile*, which means it can curl around things and hold on tightly. This is useful for a monkey who spends its life high in the branches, and who often has to use its hands to pick food.

The **wildebeest** (also called the gnu) lives on the hot, grassy plains of Africa. Flies are an ever-present problem. The wildebeest uses its long, hairy tail (number 3) as a fly-swat to keep them away.

Now you see it . . .

In the picture opposite, three animals show up at once, brightly colored in yellows and reds. They stand out like "sore thumbs" among the browns and greens of their surroundings, almost as if they want to be noticed. They are easily spotted by, say, a hungry predator. ***Why do you suppose this is?*** *(Notice the roadsigns in the background – they are brightly colored, too.)*

Look more closely at the picture. Can you see another three animals? These are "masters of disguise." They are camouflaged, which means they share the same colors as their surroundings and so remain hidden. ***Can you find them?*** *They have something to hide from – perhaps it's that hungry predator again!*

Which one is the wasp?

Some animals are not dangerous, but they look as if they are. Two of these animals look like wasps, but only one is a real wasp. This is a form of defense called "mimicry." Wasps have stings and are dangerous to animals, who avoid them. These animals usually avoid the harmless insects shown here, too. ***Can you tell which is the real wasp, and which are the mimics?***

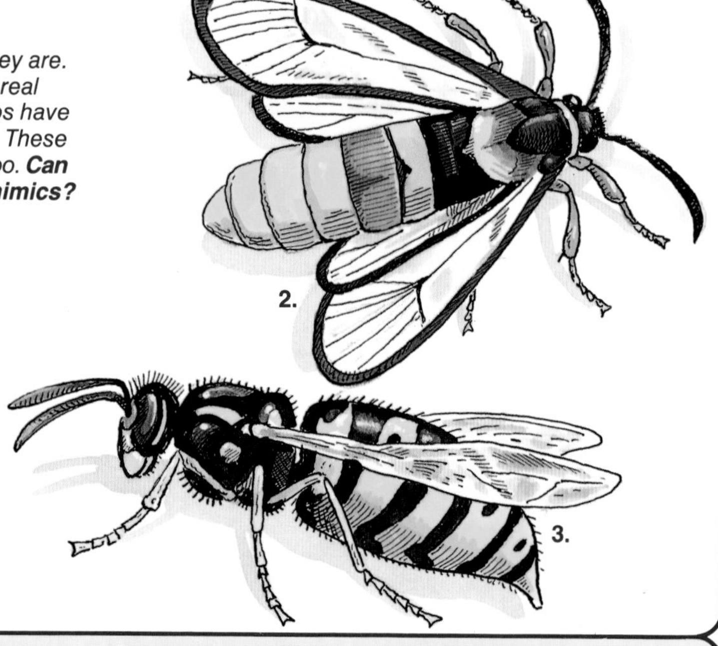

ANSWERS

WHICH ONE IS THE WASP?

1. No, this is not a wasp. It's a **hoverfly**. Unlike the wasp, it has short antennae (feelers), a darting and hovering flight, and doesn't make a buzzing sound.
2. No, this isn't a wasp either. It's a **clearwing moth**. It has smaller eyes and a hairier tail than the real wasp.
3. Yes, this is the **wasp**. Notice its large eyes, two narrow wings – and the sting in its tail!

ANSWER: STAND OUT

Bright colors spell danger! The yellow and red roadsigns warn of danger – the road ahead is flooded. Some animals use these colors as warnings too. The yellow striped hornet has a poisonous sting to defend itself. The red salamander's flesh tastes horrible, and its colors warn predators not to eat it. The yellow and black cinnabar moth caterpillar also has flesh with a bitter taste. Any bird trying to eat it is at once sick!

ANSWER: STAY HIDDEN

The odd-looking "twig" is really a looper caterpillar. When danger is near it stops looping along, head to tail, and stays still like a piece of wood, hoping not to be noticed. Hiding in the reeds is a bird, the bittern. It points its beak skywards and sways with the wind, trying to look like the reed stems. And the brown "leaf" is really a peacock butterfly. Its wings are folded, hiding the bright eye-spots (like those on a peacock's tail) on the upper sides of its wings.

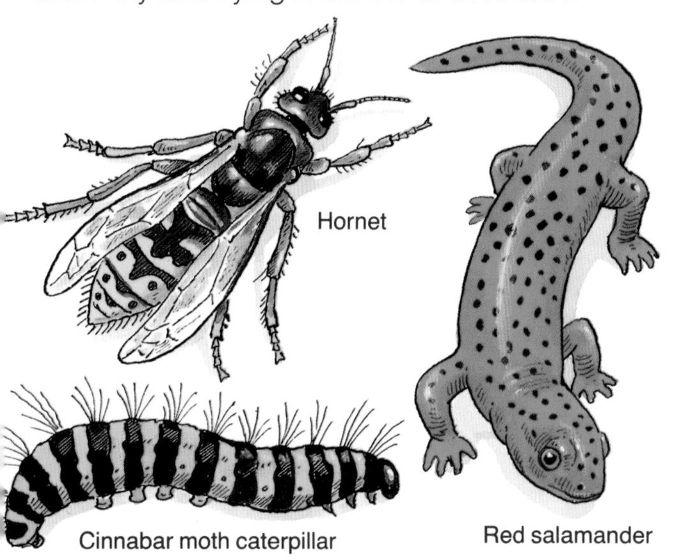

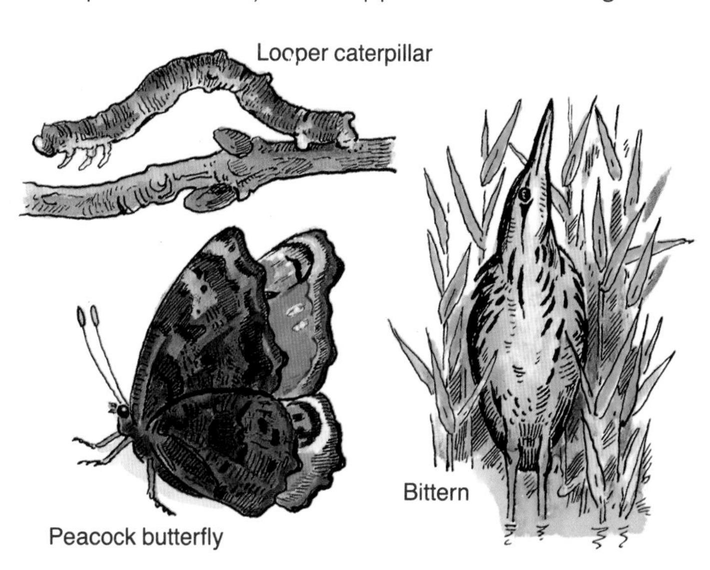

Living together

In nature, not every creature fends for itself. Some animals live together and help each other. Usually these are groups of the same kind of animal, such as starlings, or wolves. But very different creatures, such as a crab and an anemone, live together too. The animal detective wants to know: why is this?

SPREADING OUT TO SEARCH

A flock of **starlings** finds food more easily than a lone starling. The flock spreads out to search. When one finds food, the others crowd round to join in the feast.

AN UNLIKELY PAIR

The **sea anemone** sticks to the shell of the **hermit crab**. It feeds on floating bits of food stirred up by the crab's claws. In return, the crab is protected by the anemone's stinging tentacles. This sort of relationship, where both partners gain, is called "**mutualism**."

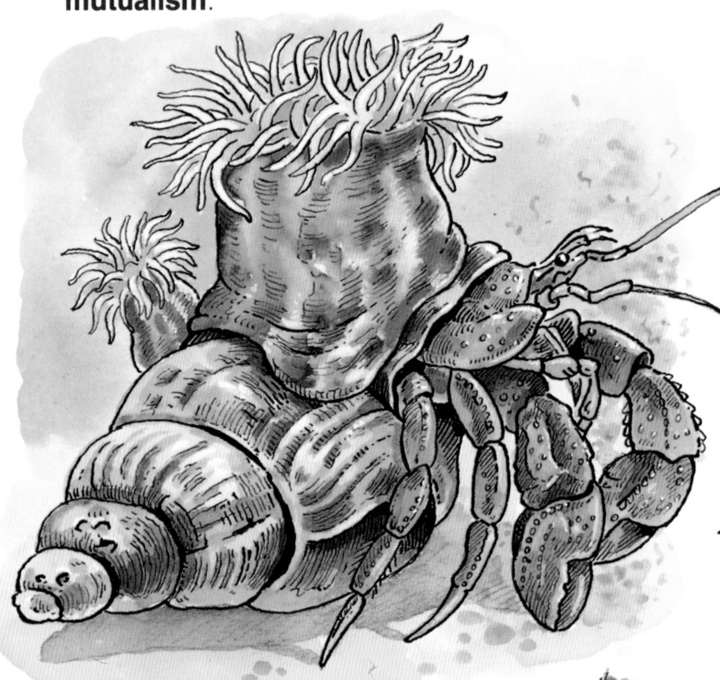

THE POWER OF THE PACK

A pack of **wolves**, hunting together, has a better chance than a lone wolf of capturing a big animal, like a moose. A large prey will feed the pack for several days, whereas capturing small prey may involve just as much effort for only a small meal.

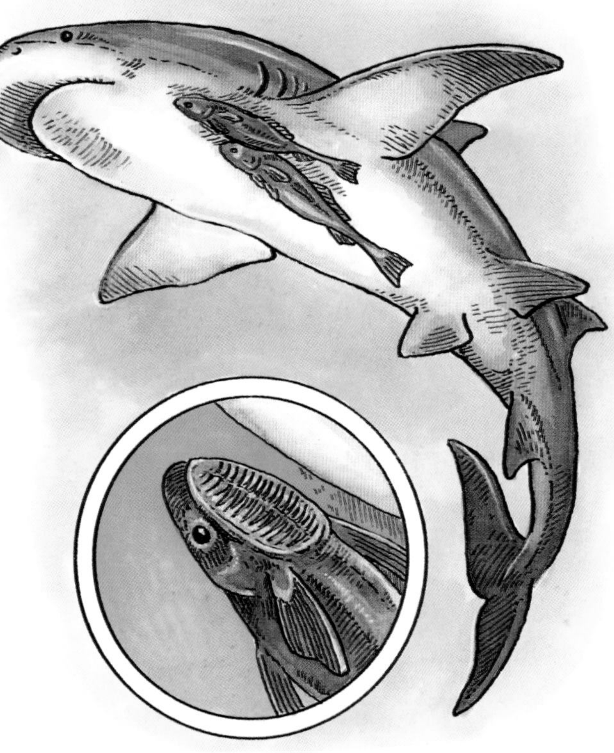

WINNER AND LOSER

The **sheep tick** lives on the **sheep** and sucks up a good meal of blood in order to live and grow. The sheep provides a safe place for the tick to live, but suffers from the irritating bite. This sort of relationship is called "**parasitism**," where there is one winner – the tick – known as the "parasite," and one loser – the sheep – known as the "host."

TWO FISH

The **remora** (sucker fish) often sticks to the underside of larger fish such as the **shark**. The remora gets a free ride, hitch-hiking on the shark, and it may eat small bits of food which break off from the shark's meal. The shark is probably not affected. This sort of relationship, where only one partner gains and the other is mostly unaffected, is called "**commensalism**."

Record breakers!

Which kind of animal lives together in the greatest numbers? *Look in the mirror for one answer – humans. The world's biggest cities, such as Mexico City and Tokyo, number more than 10 million people.*
Termites live together in nests of five million or more. In each nest there is a large, winged "queen" that lays up to 30,000 eggs each day. These are fertilized by the "king" termite. Cleaning the nest and collecting food are jobs carried out by the "worker" termites. The large-jawed "soldier" termites defend the nest. Everyone has their job in the termite society.

Food chains and webs

A herbivore eats a plant. A carnivore eats the herbivore. Another carnivore eats the first carnivore ... and soon there is a long list of who eats who. This is called a "food chain." Does a food chain ever end? Read these pages to find out.

A THREE-LINK CHAIN

A peccary grubs around on the Amazon forest floor, looking for plant food such as roots and seeds. A jaguar dashes from the undergrowth, kills the peccary with a bite to its throat, and settles down to eat its prey. This is a three-link food chain, written so:

Roots and seeds → Peccary → Jaguar

JOINING CHAINS INTO WEBS

In nature, animals rarely eat just one kind of food. The dhole, an Asian wild dog, is a carnivore. It hunts in packs and eats deer and other large animals. But it will also eat mice, lizards, beetles and even berries. Now, the lizard it eats may have fed on beetles. The mouse it eats may have gobbled up berries. If we draw in all these links, the separate food chains become joined together in a "food web."

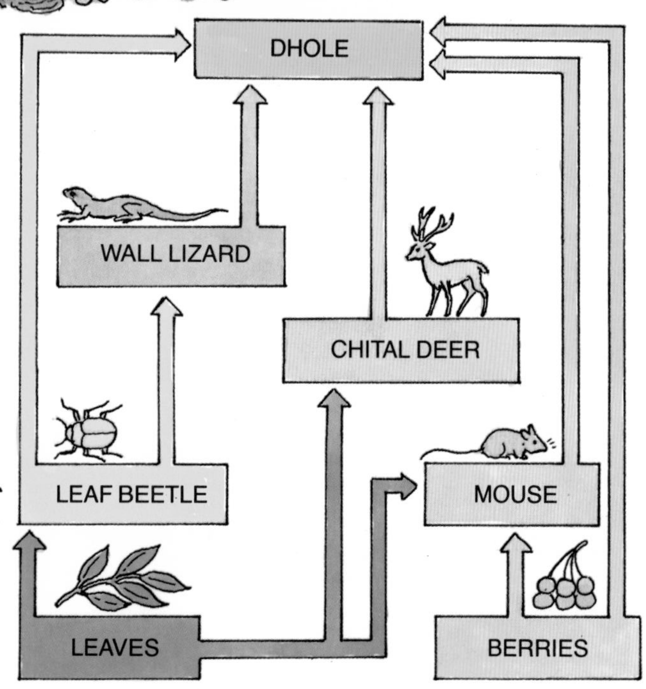

NATURE'S RE-CYCLERS

What happens at the end of a food chain? Is there ever an end? In a way, yes. For example, a big, powerful animal like a rhino is unlikely to be preyed on by a carnivore. But what happens when the rhino gets old or sick? Then another group of animals move in. These are the scavengers that eat dead bodies.

1. The rhino is old and weak. It can no longer defend itself.

2. Almost before it is dead, the scavengers arrive. Vultures peck at the rhino's flesh and hyaenas crack its bones.

3. Bits of flesh, bone and skin are left. They rot away, back into the earth.

4. Later, a plant grows on the spot, using nutrients from the soil that came from the rhino's body. A gazelle eats the plant. The food chain begins again!

Make your own food web

Can you make these common pond animals into a food web chart? Trace each animal onto thick paper or thin card, color it and cut it out. Arrange the cut outs in groups on a sheet of card: plants at the bottom, herbivores in the middle, carnivores on top, and scavengers to one side. Then move them around, depending on what they eat, to make a food web (like the one on the left). Stick them down and draw in the arrows. **Which animal is king of the pond, the "top carnivore?"** (Turn to page 36 to see if you've arrived at the right answer.)

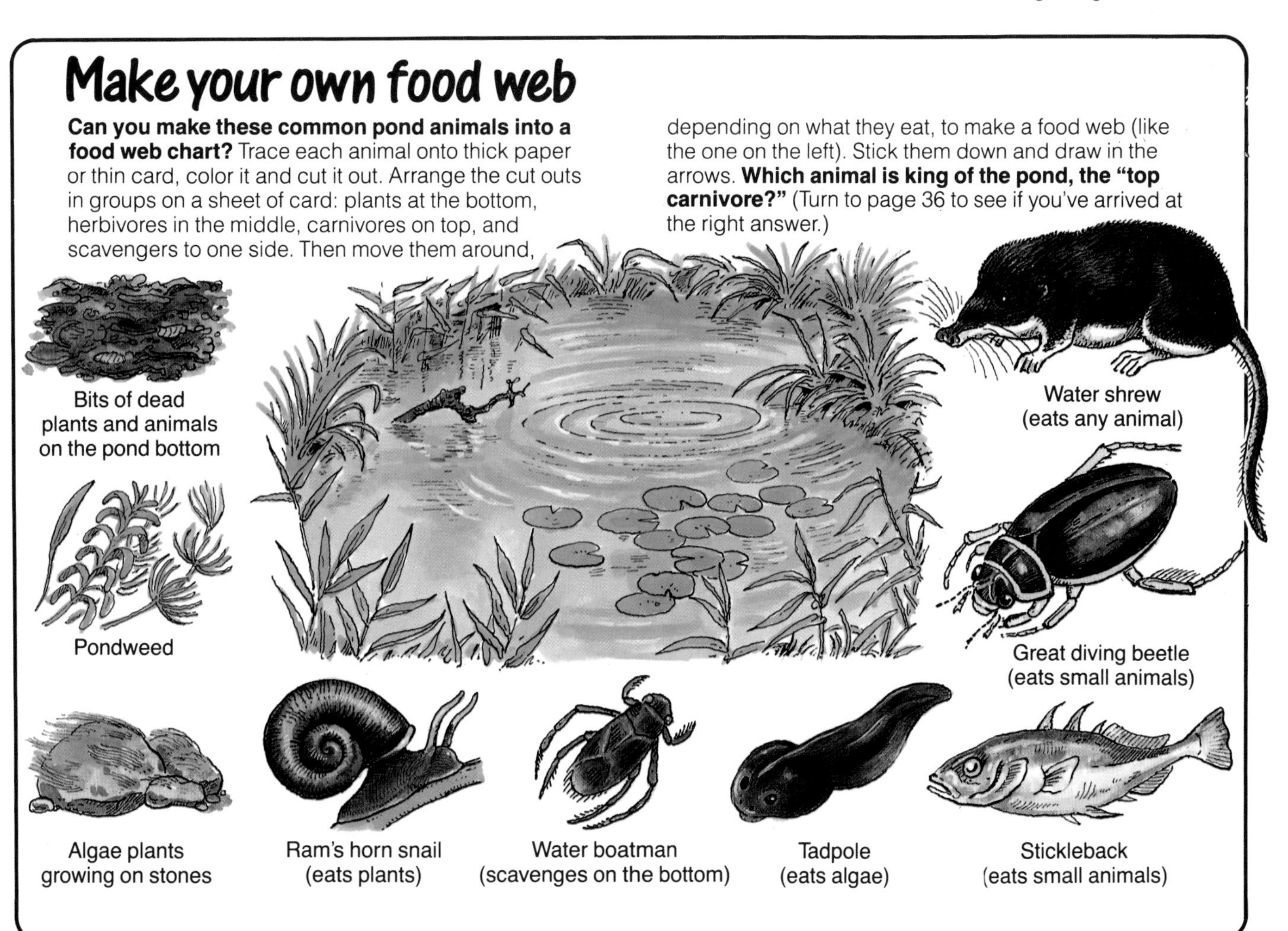

A sea of sand

Deserts may be hot, or cold, or sandy, or rocky – but they are all dry. The camel is the ideal desert animal. People have trained and used camels for hundreds of years, to carry themselves and their goods from place to place across the desert. Through evolution the camel has adapted in many ways to life in dry, often dusty, places.

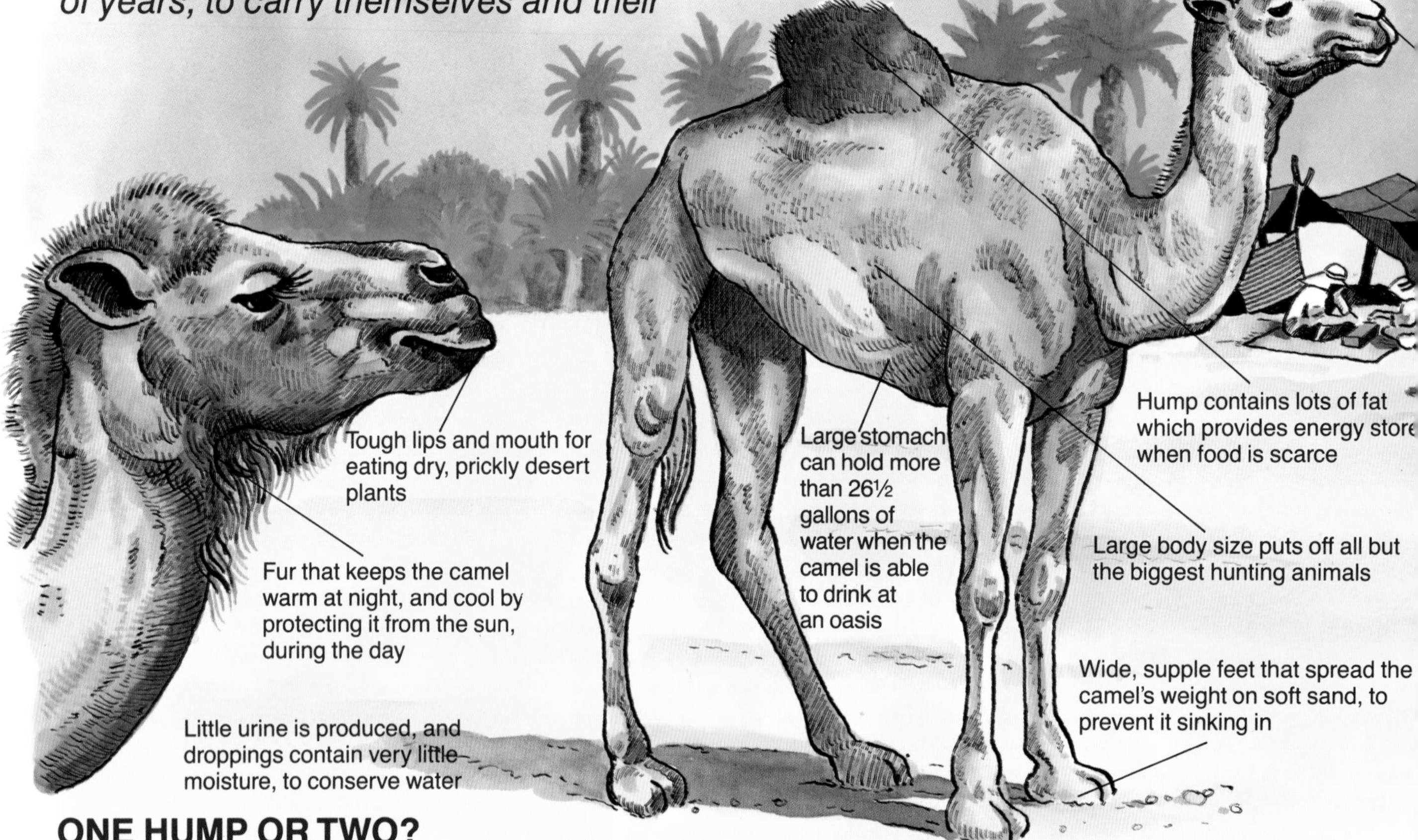

ONE HUMP OR TWO?

There are two types of camel, one-humped and two-humped. The **dromedary** (Arabian) came originally from the Middle East, but has been taken by people to other places, such as Australia where it now breeds. The **Bactrian camel** lives in Central Asia, mainly Mongolia. **Do you know which has one hump, and which has two?** (The picture above gives a clue.)

ANSWERS

SIGNS IN THE SAND

1. A wandering **beetle** forms two "tramlines" with its legs. Between the lines is a flattened strip where its body has rubbed over the sand.
2. The **kit fox's** four claws and toe pads show clearly, with a main "sole" pad in the middle. Each front foot has five toes, but one of these is too high above the ground to leave a mark.
3. These curious "waves" are made by the **sidewinder**, a type of rattlesnake. It moves sideways in a series of loops, pushing up small furrows each time it touches the sand.
4. These are the paw marks of the **jack rabbit**, which is actually a type of hare. When running, it lands on its front paws, thumps down its back ones on either side of them, and leaps away again.

ONE HUMP OR TWO?

The people in the main picture are Arabs, and their camel has one hump. So if you guessed that the camel is the Dromedary, or Arabian, camel you were right! Dromedaries have one hump, Bactrians have two humps.

Signs in the sand

Sand is excellent for showing tracks and signs of animals (provided it's not too windy!). Here are some creatures from the south-western deserts of North America. ***Can you match them to their marks in the sand?***

Make your own fennec ears!

The fennec fox is a desert-dweller from North Africa. Its enormous ears help it to detect the soft scratchings and scrapings of the small animals it preys on. They also help to keep it cool in the desert heat, as body heat escapes through the large surface of each ear.

You can make your own fennec fox ears by cutting ear shapes out of thick paper or thin card, and curving and glueing them as shown. When finished, hold the fox ears on the sides of your head just behind your own ears and listen carefully. Hear how they collect and bounce sounds into your own ears, letting you pick up the smallest noises.

Curve "ears" and glue onto bases. Each base should have a hole that slots round your own ear.

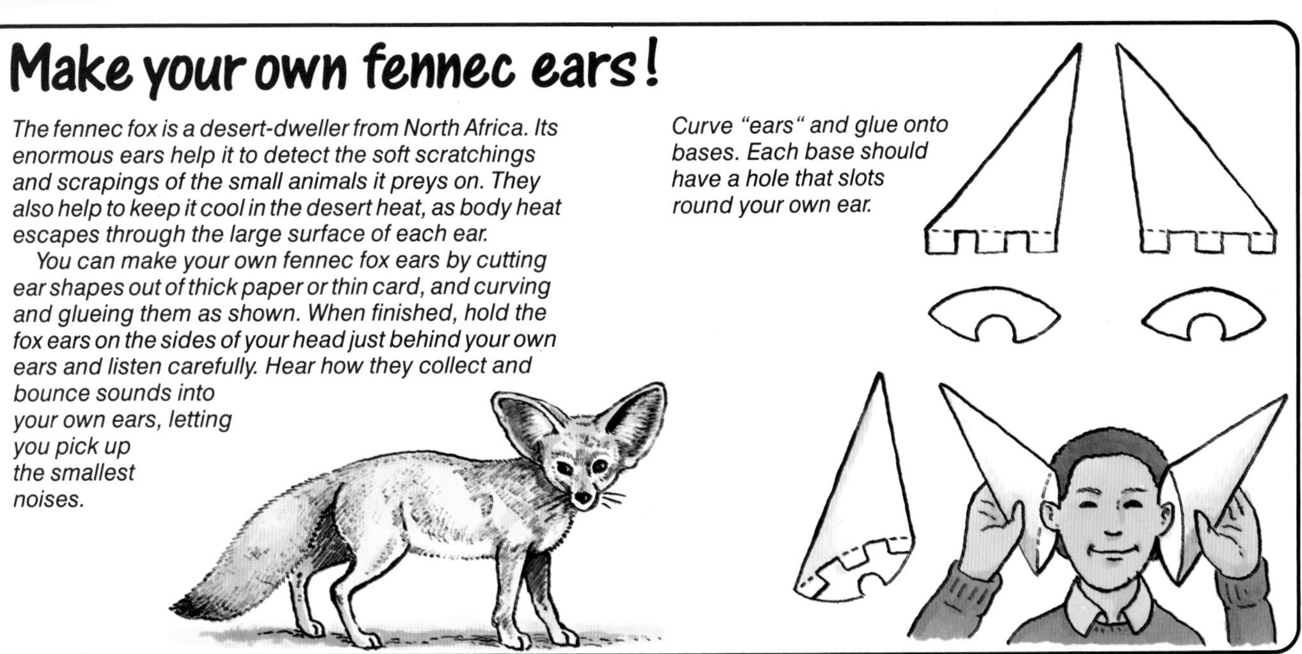

The same – but different

Look closely at these three sea animals. They all have smooth, streamlined bodies for swimming, and fins or flippers for steering. But inside, they are very different. The tuna is a fish. The dolphin is a mammal from the whale group. The sea lion is a mammal from the carnivore group. They look similar because they lead similar lives. This type of resemblance, developing over millions of years, is called ***convergent evolution****.*

BOTTLE-NOSED DOLPHIN

The dolphin swims by thrashing its tail up and down (a fish's tail fin goes from side to side). It is warm-blooded, breathes air, gives birth to live baby dolphins and feeds them on milk.

BLUEFIN TUNA

This super-fast fish grows to more than 13 feet long and swims at 43 miles per hour. It is cold-blooded, breathes through gills, is covered with scales, and lays eggs.

CALIFORNIAN SEA LION

Like the dolphin, the sea lion is a mammal that breathes air and feeds its babies on milk. Dolphins have lost their fur during evolution, but the sea lion has a thick, waterproof coat of fur.

ANSWERS

NO RELATION!
The **horseshoe bat's** fur and warm blood can mean only one thing – it's a mammal. The wing membrane is held out by very long finger bones.

The **peregrine falcon's** feathers identify it straight away as a bird. Each wing is supported mainly by arm bones.
Six legs show that the **dragonfly** is an insect. Its super-thin wings are outgrowths from its thorax (middle section), supported by thick, hard veins.

Digging in the garden

Notice the similarity between these animal's feet and the garden fork. All are specialized for digging. Often, humans design something, only to find out that nature has beaten them to it.

Giant pangolin (scaly anteater). Digs its way into ant and termite nests, and also digs a burrow in which to raise its young.

Mole. Uses its front feet for digging burrows in the soil, to find worms, slugs and other juicy food.

Garden fork

Similar, but not related

The three animals below have wings and are good fliers. But having wings doesn't necessarily mean they are closely related. It's another case of convergent evolution! **To which animal groups do they belong?** (Look back to pages 6 and 7 to remind yourself about animal groups.)

PEREGRINE FALCON
Warm-blooded, covered with feathers, and a deadly hunter of smaller birds such as pigeons.

HORSESHOE BAT
A warm-blooded, furry flier that catches insects on the wing.

DRAGONFLY
Four shimmering wings, six legs, and two enormous eyes to spot small flies.

At the ends of the Earth

The coldest places on our planet are the "ends" of the Earth – the frozen-over Arctic Ocean, around the North Pole, and the great ice cap covering the continent of Antarctica, at the South Pole. Animals living in either of these places must survive bone-chilling winds and icy temperatures of minus 60°F or lower. These conditions would kill an animal from the tropics in minutes. How are polar animals protected against such cold?

FEATHERS AND BLUBBER

Penguins live in the southern half of the world, on Antarctica and ocean islands. They cannot fly, but they swim well. Their feathers are not "feathery" at all. They are straight and narrow, more like fur. Under the skin is a thick layer of fatty substance called *blubber*. The feathers and blubber keep the cold out, and the penguin's body warmth in.

FUR AND FAT

The polar bear lives in the frozen wastes of the Arctic. It is the largest land carnivore in the world, at up to 10 feet long and weighing just over ½ ton. Its body is completely covered by thick white fur, except for its nose, eyes and parts of its feet. This animal also has a thick layer of fat under its skin, to keep out the coldest wind and water.

Whose feet?

Two of the feet here belong to animals on these two pages. You probably recognize the third one. ***Why are they all similar?***

WHO'S HIDING IN THE SNOW?

In places where there is much snow such as the Arctic, Antarctic and northern parts of Canada, USSR, Japan, and Europe, many animals have white fur or feathers for at least part of the year. Some need it to stay hidden from their enemies, others to help catch their prey. **Can you work out which of the animals shown here are the hunters and which are the hunted?**

ANSWERS

WHOSE FEET?

1. This is the paw of a polar bear. It is wide and strong, and has thick fur between its toes.
2. This is the foot of a ptarmigan. It too is very broad, with wide toes and many tough feathers.
3. This is a human's foot inside a thick boot, and with a snowshoe fixed underneath.

Broad feet help an animal to walk over soft snow without sinking in (like those of the camel on desert sand, page 20). Fur, or feathers, help to prevent the creature slipping on ice. Humans use snowshoes, with their broad design and criss-cross surface, to do the same thing. Once again, people have copied nature's designs.

WHO'S HIDING IN THE SNOW?

In summer, the **stoat's** fur is chestnut brown. In winter it turns white, so that this small hunter can be camouflaged as it creeps up on its prey of voles, mice, rabbits and small birds. In its white winter coat, the stoat is also called the ermine.

Crouching in a small hollow is an **Arctic hare**, hiding from its enemies. In the far north such as northern Scandinavia, this animal has a white winter coat for more than half the year. But in less northerly regions such as Ireland, where there is hardly any snow, it never grows a white winter coat.

The **ptarmigan's** winter plumage is all white, except for a few dark tail feathers. In spring, the white feathers molt (fall out) and brown ones grow. The bird is then camouflaged for summer, too, creeping among bushes and rocks, out of the way of any predator.

Perched on a low branch, motionless and unnoticed, is the snowy owl. A nature expert would know that this snowy owl is a female. The male is almost pure white. Both are fierce hunters.

Teeming tropical forests

Damp, tropical forests have everything that an animal could want. There's warmth, moisture, and plant food galore or, if you are a carnivore, other animals galore! Tropical forests are ideal environments for living things. In a patch of tropical forest 3½ miles square there may be 400 kinds of birds, 100 different reptiles and tens of thousands of insect species. Animal life is organized around the plant life, which is in three main layers: on the ground, in the lower branches, and in the green, sunlit canopy.

THE CANOPY, LAYER OF PLENTY

Giant forest trees stand 164 feet or more tall, stretching up towards the sun. Their leaves, blossoms and fruits provide food for thousands of animals, such as monkeys, birds, bats, snakes and butterflies.

THE UNDERSTORY, A SHADOWY WORLD

Young trees and smaller tree species, such as palms, struggle to grow in gaps between the giants. In this shady world of branches and creepers live climbing lizards and snakes, moths and other insects, spiders, small birds and climbing mammals.

THE FOREST FLOOR, DIM AND DAMP

Down on the ground, the air is still, dark and dank. Fallen trees decay in the gloom, and there are few bushes or flowers. Here live tapirs, forest deer, armadilloes, termites and ants, and worms of every shape and size.

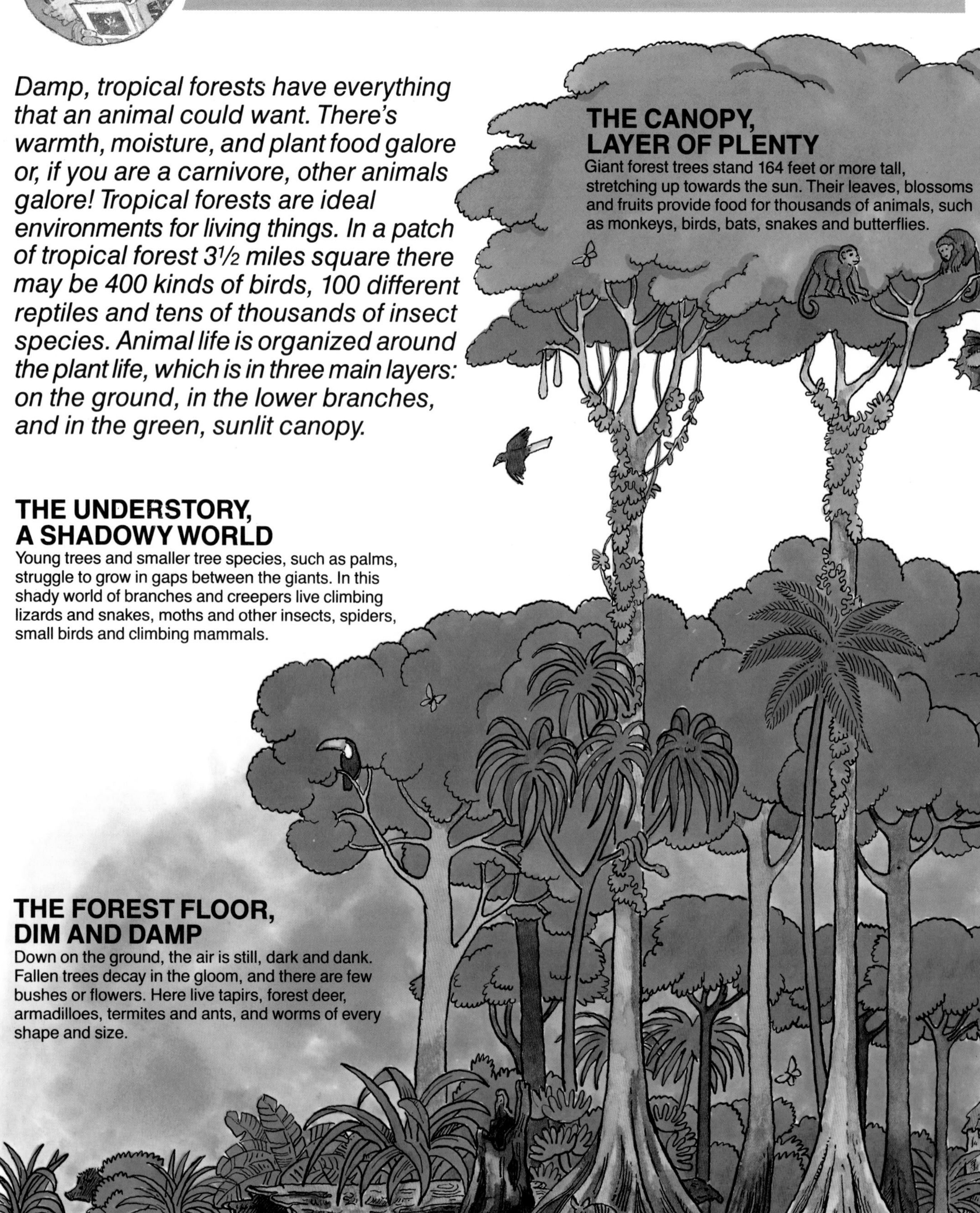

Which forest layer?

*These South American animals live in tropical forests. **But in which layer?** The clues about their body shape and food should help you to detect where they live.*

Tapir. A shy, heavily-built, hoofed animal that eats leaves and shoots.

Emerald boa. A snake that feeds on birds, bats and small mammals. It is colored bright green for camouflage.

Two-toed sloth. An amazing animal that spends its life hanging upside down from shady branches, eating leaves and fruit.

JUNGLE – OR FOREST?

People sometimes call forests "jungles." The word conjures up an image of dense tangles of ground plants, creepers, bushes and trees, which must be hacked away at every step. In fact, deep in the forest, there is little undergrowth. The light is too dim for many ground plants to grow. Sometimes you can walk freely among the tree trunks. "Jungle" grows at the edges of the forest, along riverbanks and roads and in clearings. Here, bushes and low plants have enough light to grow in a thick, matted, tangled ... jungle.

ANSWERS

WHICH FOREST LAYER?

The heavy, hoofed **tapir** cannot climb trees. It lives on the forest floor where it eats low-growing leaves and shoots

The **two-toed sloth** moves slowly through the branches, eating the leaves and fruit in the understory and lower canopy. At up to 18 lbs in weight, it is too heavy to climb the topmost twigs.

The **emerald boa's** green scales hide it well as it glides through the leaves of the canopy. It sneaks up on a small animal, strikes with a bite, squeezes the victim to death in its coils, and swallows it whole.

At home in the water

Here is a person fully dressed for diving. Each piece of equipment helps its owner to swim and dive underwater. Yet animals that are at home in the water already have many of these features, "built-in" to their own bodies, as you can see here.

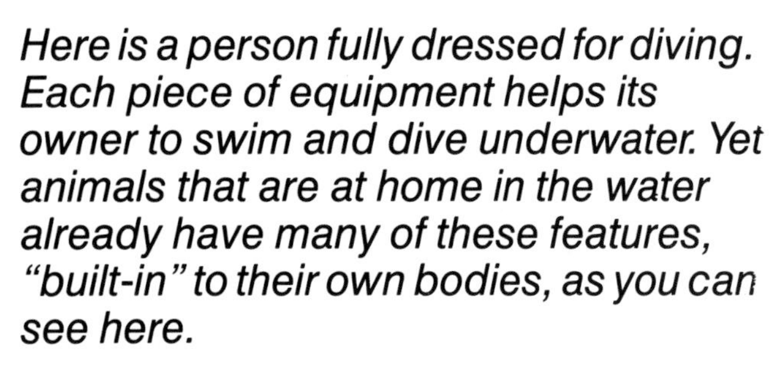

BLOOD FOR AN AQUALUNG

The **Weddell seal** of Antarctica can stay underwater for more than an hour! In proportion to its size, it has much more blood than a human. In its blood there is much more of the oxygen-carrying substance, *haemoglobin*. When the seal dives, its blood, carrying oxygen, flows mainly to its brain and muscles, so that the oxygen is used most efficiently.

THE SEAL'S "DRYSUIT"

The **fur seal** has two types of fur that make, not a wetsuit, but a "drysuit." The dense undercoat has many short, fine hairs. The overcoat has longer, thicker, less numerous "guard hairs." Oil from glands in the skin make all the hairs water-repellant. So outside it may be cold and wet, but inside, the fur seal is warm and dry!

FOUR EYES ARE BETTER THAN TWO

The strange **four-eyed fish** of Central America has built-in "goggles." It has two eyes, but each eye is in two parts. The upper part sees clearly in air, and the lower part in water. This fish swims at the surface, on the double-lookout for food.

FLIPPER POWER

Evolution has modified the **manatee's** arms into flippers. It has a flipper-like tail, too, which waves up and down to push the animal forward. This odd creature is also known as the "sea cow" since it eats underwater grasses and seaweeds.

Sharp and to the point

The swordfish's harpoon-like "sword" is thought to be used for feeding. This creature swims at speed through a school of smaller fish, thrashing with its head. The "sword" grazes some fish and may even stick into others. The swordfish then swims round and returns to eat the dead and injured victims.

Make your own webbed feet

A fish's fin, a seal's flipper, an otter's webbed foot, and a penguin's wing are all similar – they have a broad surface to push backwards against the water, propelling the animal along. When they are pulled forwards, they can be folded or twisted to reduce resistance to the water. You can make a "webbed foot" – with your hand! Put a small plastic bag over one hand, and hold its opening tightly around your wrist with your other hand. Try "swimming" in a sink or bathtub. Spread and stiffen your fingers on the backward stroke, to make the "webs" open out. On the forward stroke, close your fingers and let them bend. See how much more power there is on the backstroke. Don't get too much water on the floor!

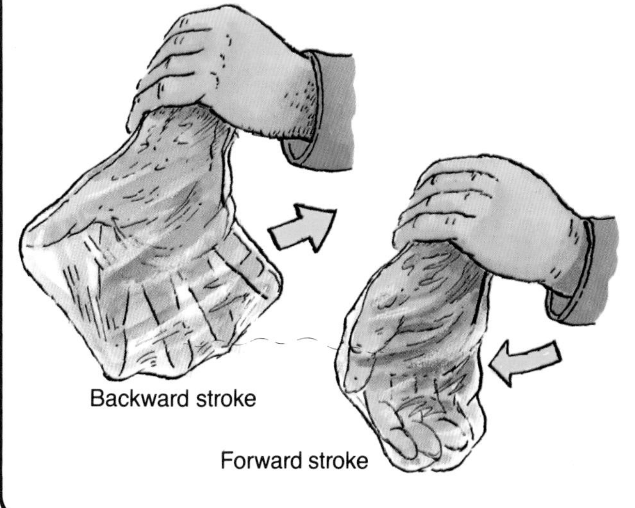

Between the tides

Imagine that you are a creature living on a seashore. When the tide is out, the sun or wind dries you up. If it rains you are covered with fresh water. When the tide comes in, you are covered with salty water, and the waves batter you to and fro. How do you survive? There are many different ways, as you can see here.

Hiding away! The **grey sea slug** is a relative of land slugs. It often follows the retreating tide so that it is not left out of water. At other times it crawls under seaweed, or hides under a rocky overhang, to remain cool and damp.

Clamping on! At high water, the **limpet** moves slowly over the rocks, grazing on seaweeds. When the tide goes out, this mollusk clamps down its shell using its powerful snail-like "foot." It grips the rock so strongly that not even the largest wave – or a curious person – can dislodge it.

Digging in! The **common shrimp** burrows into sand as the tide goes out, to stay safe and moist. This crustacean usually comes out to feed only at night, when it is cool. So if it is stranded by the tide, it has more chance of surviving.

Shutting up! The **barnacle** is a very strange creature: it cements its head to a rock, lives upside down in its shell, and kicks food into its mouth! As the tide goes out, and the barnacle is no longer covered by sea water, it shuts the "door" of its shell, to keep out sunshine and rain.

ANSWERS

NATURE'S THROW-AWAYS

1. A "cuttlebone," the internal shell of the **cuttlefish**, a relative of the octopus.
2. Empty egg-cases of the **whelk**, a large sea snail.
3. An empty egg case of a **skate** or ray, or perhaps a dogfish, often called a "mermaid's purse."
4. The shell of a **sea urchin**, after its spines have fallen off.

HOW MANY LEGS?

The **octopus** has eight arms. Each one has a row of suckers underneath that grasp fish and other prey. It usually lives in deeper water, but it may be stranded in a rock pool by the tide.

The **crab** has ten "legs," although the first pair is actually its pincers! It also has two pairs of antennae (short feelers) and three sets of mouthparts for sifting food.

This seashore **centipede** has 10 legs – give or take a few. It hunts tiny animals in among seaweed and stones.

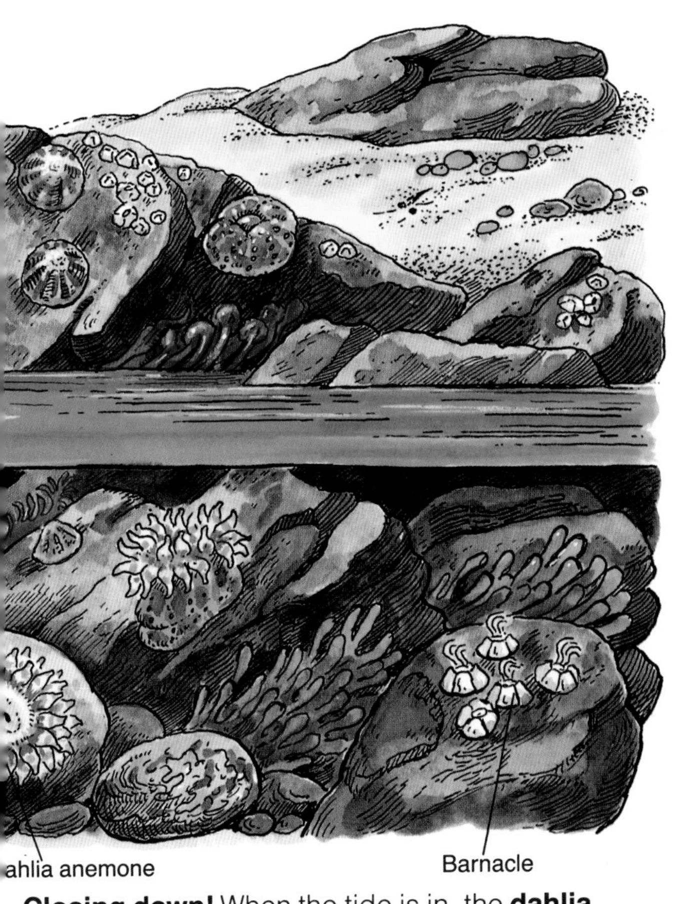

Closing down! When the tide is in, the **dahlia anemone** waves its tentacles in the water to catch and poison small creatures. As the tide retreats, it folds its tentacles into its rubbery "stalk" so that it looks like an overgrown winegum.

How many legs ?

Some shore animals have a bewildering array of legs, tentacles, feelers and other limbs. ***How many do these animals possess?*** *There is a clue for each one.*

Octopus, a mollusk
(Clue: In geometry, an *octagon* has eight sides.)

Velvet swimming crab, a decapod crustacean
(Clue: In athletics, the *decathlon* has ten events.)

Strigamia centipede
(Clue: 100 years make a *century*.)

Natures throw-aways

Beachcombing is fascinating for the animal detective. There are so many strange objects along the "strand line", washed up by the waves. ***Can you identify these common finds?***

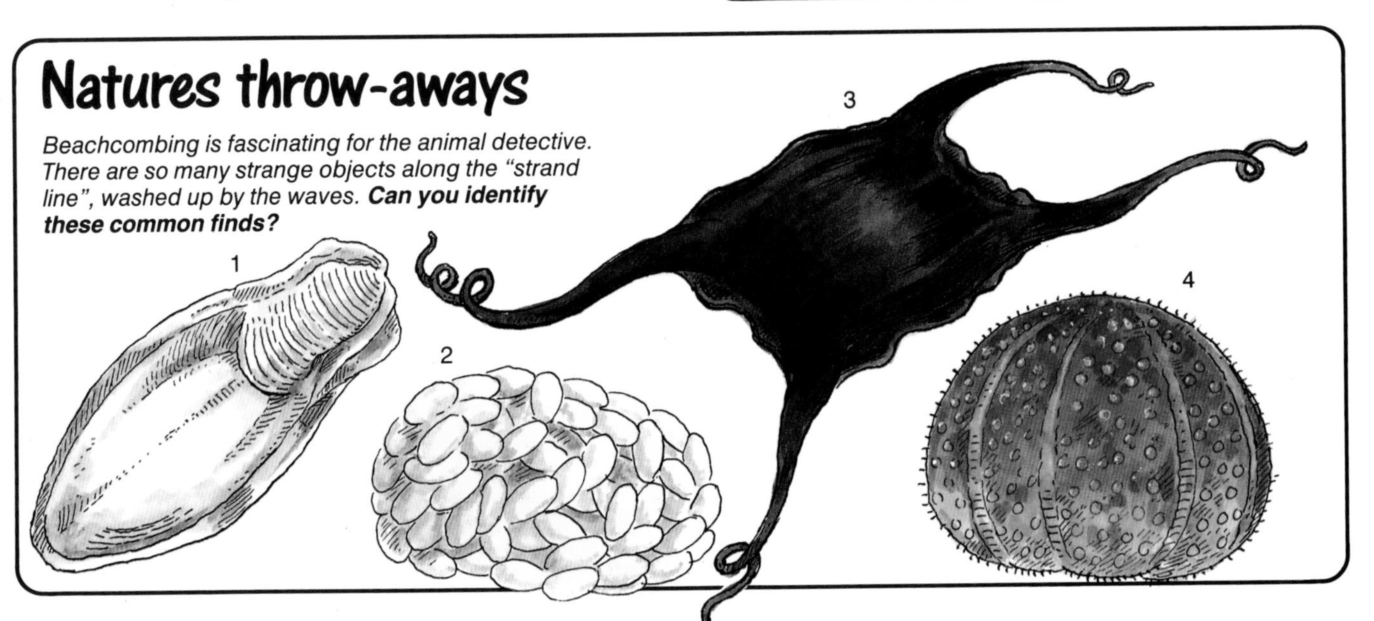

Living in the city

In cities all over the world, animals make their homes – from sparrows in gardens to seagulls on rubbish tips, from storks nesting on rooftops to rats in sewers. Animals make their homes indoors too: there are spiders behind skirting boards, bats in attics and toads in cellars. Look at the town garden below. The animals can't be seen – but look at all the signs and traces they have left! ***Which creatures on the opposite page made them?***

ANSWERS

IN THE CITY
1. House martin's nest
2. Pigeon's droppings
3. Cabbages eaten by caterpillars of large white butterfly
4. Earthworm's soil casts
5. Garden spider's web
6. Grey squirrel's food store
7. Rabbit's droppings
8. Dustbin upset by fox

NESTS IN THE ROOF

Nest 1 was made by the brown rat, which climbs well and thrives in places where humans live.

Nest 2 belongs to a swallow. In spring it would contain about five pale, speckled eggs.

Nest 3 was made by a colony of wasps. They scrape wood in their jaws and chew it with their saliva to make the "paper."

Rabbit. Comes in from nearby wasteland or park to feast in the vegetable patch, and often leaves small, round droppings.

Large white butterfly. Its caterpillars eat leaves, and are very partial to cabbages. They are often called "cabbage whites."

Garden spider. Often spins its web near a street lamp or chink in the curtains, to catch flies and moths attracted to the light.

Earthworm. Eats soil as it tunnels along, and squirts the soil from its rear end onto the surface as a squiggly "cast."

Grey squirrel. Digs holes to bury nuts and other food, but often forgets to bury its store, or forgets where it is!

Nests in the roof

Imagine exploring a roof space or loft and finding these three nests. ***Can you match each one to its builder?***

1. An untidy heap of grass, straw, bits of string, fluff and brownish hairs.

2. A neat cup-shaped nest of mud and feathers, strengthened with straw and plant stalks.

3. A beautifully intricate nest made of a papery substance, with a small entrance hole.

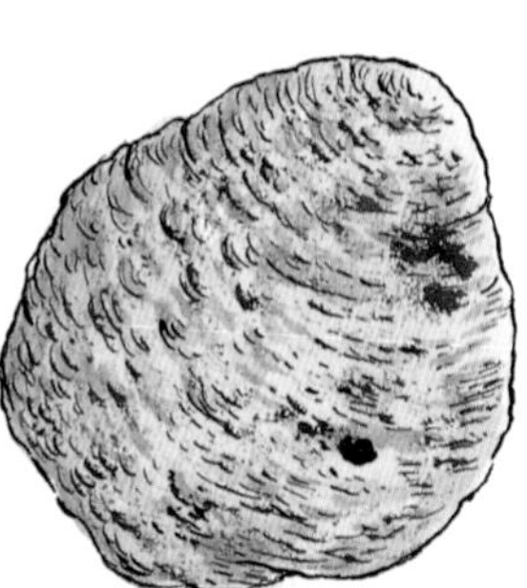

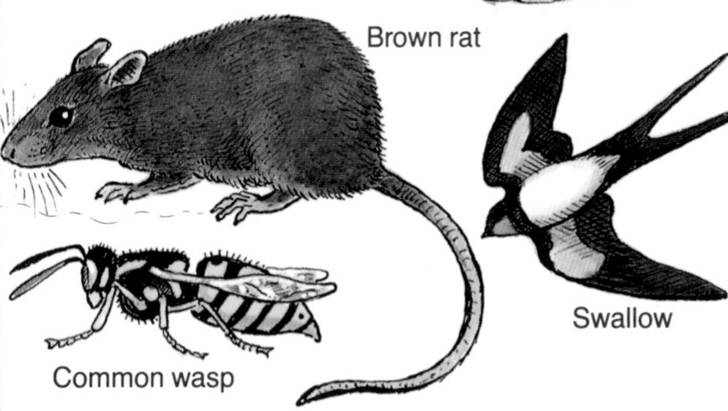

Pigeon. Roosts at night on a convenient ledge, preferably somewhere warm, where it leaves its droppings.

House martin. Makes a half-cup-shaped nest of mud as a home for its chicks.

Fox. Roams through gardens at night, eating what it can and even tipping over dustbins to look for left-over scraps.

Animals in danger

It does not take an expert nature detective to know that some animals in our world are in danger of ***extinction*** *– of dying out and disappearing for ever. Conservationists think that every day, somewhere in the world, an animal species becomes extinct. Here are some larger, well-known animals that are in danger of extinction. But there are thousands of others, and plants too.* ***Do you know which animal, above all others, is responsible for endangering animal species?***

SUMATRAN RHINO

There may be fewer than 200 of these animals left in the mountain forests of South East Asia. Some are killed for their horns, which are ground up and used as traditional medicines. Scientists say the horns contain no helpful drugs, but the people who use the medicines believe that they are helpful. Old traditions do not die out as quickly as the rhinos.

GIANT PANDA

The giant panda is a world symbol of conservation. It lives in the mountain forests of central and western China, and eats bamboo leaves. But trees are being cut down and villages and farmlands are expanding in the area, so there is less and less forest left for the pandas. There are only about 1,000 giant pandas left in the wild.

CALIFORNIAN CONDOR

The last female Californian condor in the wild died in 1986. The future of these great birds now depends on a handful kept in zoos. It is hoped that they will breed and build up in number so that some can be released back into the wild. The next few years are critical.

A SUCCESS STORY

In 1972, only 1,800 Indian tigers were thought to survive, and their numbers were dwindling fast. Some 15 special tiger reserves were set up. Now there are about 4,000 Indian tigers – a success story for conservationists. However, other types or **subspecies**, of the tiger species are still very rare.

BIRDWING BUTTERFLY

The world's largest butterfly is also one of the rarest. It is Queen Alexandra's birdwing, from Papua New Guinea. Cutting down forests for timber and to clear land to plant oil palm trees, has made this beautiful insect very rare.

THE FINAL ANSWER?

Many animals are in danger because of a large mammal that calls itself ***Homo sapiens***. This means "Wise Man" – the human being. Yet many of the things we humans do are hardly wise. We depend on animals and plants for food, shelter, and useful goods such as medicines. We also like to watch and admire animals. In cutting down forests for wood, clearing land for houses, factories and crops, and polluting the land, sea and air, we are slowly destroying our wildlife.

A good detective looks at facts and evidence. The evidence is clear: animals are dying out. We must look to the future, and do what we can to help them. You can help animals, and all wildlife, in many ways. Join a conservation organization. Ask if you can do a conservation project at school. Find out about rare animals from books and magazines, and get your family and friends interested. Help your local conservation volunteers to plant a woodland or clear a rubbish-filled pond. Conservation, like some other good habits, begins at home.

Quiz time

The natural world provides us with many clues that can be used to work out why creatures look and behave as they do. Here are a few more animal puzzles that you can solve by looking back through this book. Knowing where to look for facts and information is part of the skill of becoming a great animal detective. You can find out more about animals from books, magazines, TV, nature holidays, keeping pets ... the rest is up to you!

THE POND FOOD WEB

The food web of pond plants and animals from page 19 should look like this:

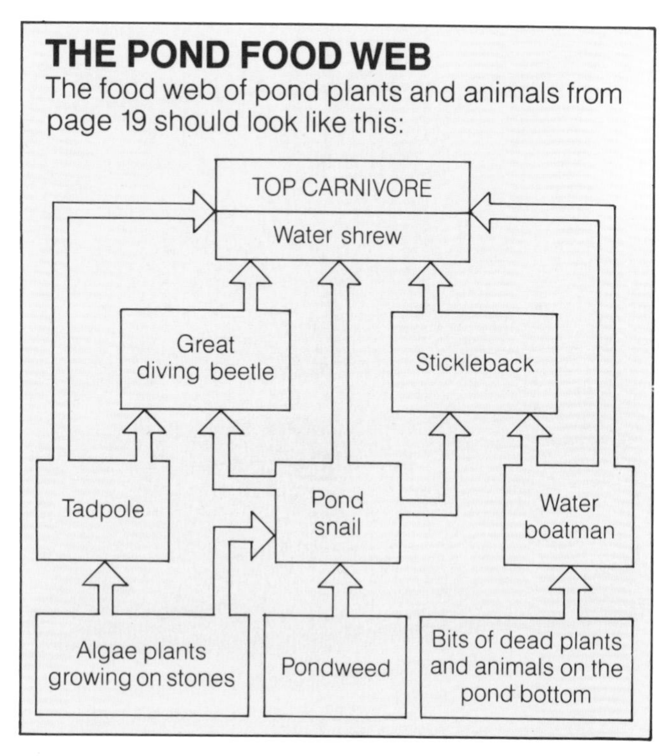

WALRUS WHEREABOUTS

The walrus is an odd animal indeed. It has limbs shaped like flippers, and thick skin with a layer of fatty blubber beneath. **What part of the world, and what habitat, do you think it lives in?** Clue: it never sees a penguin!

Which group of animals?

The animal detective must be careful when identifying which group an animal belongs to. Here are some tricky ones. ***After looking back to page 6, can you work out which group each one is in?***

Platypus. This furry Australian animal lays hard-shelled eggs in a hole in the riverbank. The young hatch out and suckle milk from their mother.

Armadillo. The body of this American animal is covered in hard, bony-looking plates and it can roll itself into a ball for protection. The mother feeds her young on milk.

Caecilian. This burrowing, worm-like African creature lays eggs in soil near a stream or pond. The eggs hatch into tadpole-shaped young that live at first in water, gradually changing to look like their parents and live on land.

WHERE WOULD THEY HIDE?

Most cats hunt by stealth. They creep close to their prey, and then suddenly rush at it. **In which surroundings do you think each of these cats lives?** Remember that camouflage helps when stalking a wary victim.

★ANSWERS★

WHICH GROUP OF ANIMALS?

Armadillo. The hard "scales" of an armadillo make it look like a reptile. But the young are fed on milk – so it must be a mammal.

Platypus. Birds and reptiles lay hard-shelled eggs, and so does the platypus. But the platypus has fur, and feeds its young on milk so, although it lays eggs, it's a mammal. Only two mammals lay eggs. The other is the echidna (spiny anteater).

Caecilian. It looks like a worm – but the way its eggs hatch into water-living tadpoles shows it is an amphibian, related to the frogs and newts.

WALRUS WHEREABOUTS

The walrus, with flippers like its cousins the seals, is suited to life in the ocean. The thick blubber is another clue: blubber is a good insulator, so the walrus probably lives in a cold ocean. Correct! The Arctic and Antarctic Oceans are cold. But penguins live in the Antarctic, and the walrus never sees them. So it must live in the Arctic Ocean. Correct again!

WHERE WOULD THEY HIDE?

Tigers have striped coats that help them blend in with the stems, bushes and grass of their forest and scrub home. They hunt at dusk or dawn, so they are even more difficult to see!

The **leopard's** spotty coat hides it well when it's lying in the dappled shade of a tree. Sometimes this cat lies on a branch and drops silently onto its prey's back.

The yellow and brown colors in the tawny fur of the **caracal** are a good match for the dry, scrubby plants and the sandy soils of its home.

Index